TRUST IN THE LORD
WITH ALL YOUR

Heart

Date : _____

Today's Verse

Lord teach me to...

I am thankful for...

Prayer Requests

Date : _____

Today's Verse

Lord teach me to...

I am thankful for...

Prayer Requests

Date : _____

Today's Verse

Lord teach me to...

I am thankful for...

Prayer Requests

Date : _____

Today's Verse

Lord teach me to...

I am thankful for...

Prayer Requests

Date : _____

Today's Verse

Lord teach me to...

I am thankful for...

Prayer Requests

Date : _____

Today's Verse

Lord teach me to...

I am thankful for...

Prayer Requests

Date : _____

Today's Verse

Lord teach me to...

I am thankful for...

Prayer Requests

Date : _____

Today's Verse

Lord teach me to...

I am thankful for...

Prayer Requests

Date : _____

Today's Verse

Lord teach me to...

I am thankful for...

Prayer Requests

Date : _____

Today's Verse

Lord teach me to...

I am thankful for...

Prayer Requests

Date : _____

Today's Verse

Lord teach me to...

I am thankful for...

Prayer Requests

Date : _____

Today's Verse

Lord teach me to...

I am thankful for...

Prayer Requests

Date : _____

Today's Verse

Lord teach me to...

I am thankful for...

Prayer Requests

Date : _____

Today's Verse

Lord teach me to...

I am thankful for...

Prayer Requests

Date : _____

Today's Verse

Lord teach me to...

I am thankful for...

Prayer Requests

Date : _____

Today's Verse

Lord teach me to...

I am thankful for...

Prayer Requests

Date : _____

Today's Verse

Lord teach me to...

I am thankful for...

Prayer Requests

Date : _____

Today's Verse

Lord teach me to...

I am thankful for...

Prayer Requests

Date : _____

Today's Verse

Lord teach me to...

I am thankful for...

Prayer Requests

Date : _____

Today's Verse

Lord teach me to...

I am thankful for...

Prayer Requests

Date : _____

Today's Verse

Lord teach me to...

I am thankful for...

Prayer Requests

Date : _____

Today's Verse

Lord teach me to...

I am thankful for...

Prayer Requests

Date : _____

Today's Verse

Lord teach me to...

I am thankful for...

Prayer Requests

Date : _____

Today's Verse

Lord teach me to...

I am thankful for...

Prayer Requests

Date : _____

Today's Verse

Lord teach me to...

I am thankful for...

Prayer Requests

Date : _____

Today's Verse

Lord teach me to...

I am thankful for...

Prayer Requests

Date : _____

Today's Verse

Lord teach me to...

I am thankful for...

Prayer Requests

Date : _____

Today's Verse

Lord teach me to...

I am thankful for...

Prayer Requests

Date : _____

Today's Verse

Lord teach me to...

I am thankful for...

Prayer Requests

Date : _____

Today's Verse

Lord teach me to...

I am thankful for...

Prayer Requests

Date : _____

Today's Verse

Lord teach me to...

I am thankful for...

Prayer Requests

Date : _____

Today's Verse

Lord teach me to...

I am thankful for...

Prayer Requests

Date : _____

Today's Verse

Lord teach me to...

I am thankful for...

Prayer Requests

Date : _____

Today's Verse

Lord teach me to...

I am thankful for...

Prayer Requests

Date : _____

Today's Verse

Lord teach me to...

I am thankful for...

Prayer Requests

Date : _____

Today's Verse

Lord teach me to...

I am thankful for...

Prayer Requests

Date : _____

Today's Verse

Lord teach me to...

I am thankful for...

Prayer Requests

Date : _____

Today's Verse

Lord teach me to...

I am thankful for...

Prayer Requests

Date : _____

Today's Verse

Lord teach me to...

I am thankful for...

Prayer Requests

Date : _____

Today's Verse

Lord teach me to...

I am thankful for...

Prayer Requests

Date : _____

Today's Verse

Lord teach me to...

I am thankful for...

Prayer Requests

Date : _____

Today's Verse

Lord teach me to...

I am thankful for...

Prayer Requests

Date : _____

Today's Verse

Lord teach me to...

I am thankful for...

Prayer Requests

Date : _____

Today's Verse

Lord teach me to...

I am thankful for...

Prayer Requests

Date : _____

Today's Verse

Lord teach me to...

I am thankful for...

Prayer Requests

Date : _____

Today's Verse

Lord teach me to...

I am thankful for...

Prayer Requests

Date : _____

Today's Verse

Lord teach me to...

I am thankful for...

Prayer Requests

Date : _____

Today's Verse

Lord teach me to...

I am thankful for...

Prayer Requests

Date : _____

Today's Verse

Lord teach me to...

I am thankful for...

Prayer Requests

Date : _____

Today's Verse

Lord teach me to...

I am thankful for...

Prayer Requests

Date : _____

Today's Verse

Lord teach me to...

I am thankful for...

Prayer Requests

Date : _____

Today's Verse

Lord teach me to...

I am thankful for...

Prayer Requests

Date : _____

Today's Verse

Lord teach me to...

I am thankful for...

Prayer Requests

Date : _____

Today's Verse

Lord teach me to...

I am thankful for...

Prayer Requests

Date : _____

Today's Verse

Lord teach me to...

I am thankful for...

Prayer Requests

Date : _____

Today's Verse

Lord teach me to...

I am thankful for...

Prayer Requests

Date : _____

Today's Verse

Lord teach me to...

I am thankful for...

Prayer Requests

Date : _____

Today's Verse

Lord teach me to...

I am thankful for...

Prayer Requests

Date : _____

Today's Verse

Lord teach me to...

I am thankful for...

Prayer Requests

Date : _____

Today's Verse

Lord teach me to...

I am thankful for...

Prayer Requests

Date : _____

Today's Verse

Lord teach me to...

I am thankful for...

Prayer Requests

Date : _____

Today's Verse

Lord teach me to...

I am thankful for...

Prayer Requests

Date : _____

Today's Verse

Lord teach me to...

I am thankful for...

Prayer Requests

Date : _____

Today's Verse

Lord teach me to...

I am thankful for...

Prayer Requests

Date : _____

Today's Verse

Lord teach me to...

I am thankful for...

Prayer Requests

Date : _____

Today's Verse

Lord teach me to...

I am thankful for...

Prayer Requests

Date : _____

Today's Verse

Lord teach me to...

I am thankful for...

Prayer Requests

Date : _____

Today's Verse

Lord teach me to...

I am thankful for...

Prayer Requests

Date : _____

Today's Verse

Lord teach me to...

I am thankful for...

Prayer Requests

Date : _____

Today's Verse

Lord teach me to...

I am thankful for...

Prayer Requests

Date : _____

Today's Verse

Lord teach me to...

I am thankful for...

Prayer Requests

Date : _____

Today's Verse

Lord teach me to...

I am thankful for...

Prayer Requests

Date : _____

Today's Verse

Lord teach me to...

I am thankful for...

Prayer Requests

Date : _____

Today's Verse

Lord teach me to...

I am thankful for...

Prayer Requests

Date : _____

Today's Verse

Lord teach me to...

I am thankful for...

Prayer Requests

Date : _____

Today's Verse

Lord teach me to...

I am thankful for...

Prayer Requests

Date : _____

Today's Verse

Lord teach me to...

I am thankful for...

Prayer Requests

Date : _____

Today's Verse

Lord teach me to...

I am thankful for...

Prayer Requests

Date : _____

Today's Verse

Lord teach me to...

I am thankful for...

Prayer Requests

Date : _____

Today's Verse

Lord teach me to...

I am thankful for...

Prayer Requests

Date : _____

Today's Verse

Lord teach me to...

I am thankful for...

Prayer Requests

Date : _____

Today's Verse

Lord teach me to...

I am thankful for...

Prayer Requests

Date : _____

Today's Verse

Lord teach me to...

I am thankful for...

Prayer Requests

Date : _____

Today's Verse

Lord teach me to...

I am thankful for...

Prayer Requests

Date : _____

Today's Verse

Lord teach me to...

I am thankful for...

Prayer Requests

Date : _____

Today's Verse

Lord teach me to...

I am thankful for...

Prayer Requests

Date : _____

Today's Verse

Lord teach me to...

I am thankful for...

Prayer Requests

Date : _____

Today's Verse

Lord teach me to...

I am thankful for...

Prayer Requests

Date : _____

Today's Verse

Lord teach me to...

I am thankful for...

Prayer Requests

Date : _____

Today's Verse

Lord teach me to...

I am thankful for...

Prayer Requests

Date : _____

Today's Verse

Lord teach me to...

I am thankful for...

Prayer Requests

Date : _____

Today's Verse

Lord teach me to...

I am thankful for...

Prayer Requests

Date : _____

Today's Verse

Lord teach me to...

I am thankful for...

Prayer Requests

Date : _____

Today's Verse

Lord teach me to...

I am thankful for...

Prayer Requests

Date : _____

Today's Verse

Lord teach me to...

I am thankful for...

Prayer Requests

Date : _____

Today's Verse

Lord teach me to...

I am thankful for...

Prayer Requests

Date : _____

Today's Verse

Lord teach me to...

I am thankful for...

Prayer Requests

Date : _____

Today's Verse

Lord teach me to...

I am thankful for...

Prayer Requests

Date : _____

Today's Verse

Lord teach me to...

I am thankful for...

Prayer Requests

Date : _____

Today's Verse

Lord teach me to...

I am thankful for...

Prayer Requests

Printed in Great Britain
by Amazon